APPLETREE PRESS

the pick of IRISH RIDDLES

an illustrated selection of
IRISH PUZZLE POEMS

PAT FAIRON

ILLUSTRATED BY PHILIP BLYTHE

Published by
Appletree Press
19-21 Alfred Street,
Belfast BT2 8DL

For permission to reproduce material the following acknowledgments are made: to the Head of the Department of Irish Folklore, University College, Dublin, for material from Schools Manuscripts; to the Secretary of the Folklore of Ireland Society for material from the journal *Bealoideas*; and to the County Museum, Armagh, for material from the Patterson Collection.

The Pick of Irish Riddles
A catalogue record for this book is available from the British Library.

ISBN 0-86281-608-4

9 8 7 6 5 4 3 2 1

Printed in Ireland

Introduction

In an oral tradition true riddles seem to offer a playful challenge to the people's conventional views of their world. They do this by describing the familiar in words and terms that make it sound magical and mysterious. Unlike some forms of the riddle, true riddles aim not to trick but to offer a fresh view of the world. To me they are poems - peoples' poetry.

Pat Fairon
Loughgall, Co. Armagh

Answers to the riddles are on page 48

A steel pig going over a bone bridge
and a brass man driving it.

EST.1921
S. EWING.
& SONS

EQUATOR
N
Urquharts Passage
Steinhaus
Route
Nelsons' Path
ICARUS
PHILIP BLYTHE '92.

It was in the river but wasn't drowned
It was in the grass but wasn't cut
It was in the shop but wasn't sold.

As white as milk but milk it's not
As green as grass but grass it's not
As red as a rose but rose it's not.
As black as ink but ink it's not.

PHILIP BLYTHE '92.

Who do I see coming through the sea
But the toy of the sun
A man with a blue coat
And a red thread in his shirt.

Big biddy from the north
Has a big mouth but can't talk
Two iron ears and can't hear
Three iron legs and can't walk.

It once was low
But now it's high
It once was wet
But now it's dry
It once was black
But now it's red
I put it upstanding
And it fell down dead.

Two brothers we are, great burdens
we bear
In which we are bitterly pressed
The truth we do speak, we are full
all the day
And empty when we go to rest.

PHILIP BLYTHE '92

When I'm old they cut me
And in a hole they put me
When I'm three months old
They come looking me quite bold
Between fire and water they
burn me
Between two irons they turn me
And when I'm stripped of my skin
They find a hole to put me in.

Hidi Hadi on the wall
Hidi Hadi got a fall
Three men and threescore
Wouldn't leave Hidi Hadi
As he was before.

Philip Blythe '92

Through a rock, through a reel
Through an old spinning wheel
Through a bag of feathers
Through an old mud wall
If that's not a riddle
There's no riddle at all.

Brothers and sisters have I none
But this man's father
Was my father's son.

Who is it?

I washed my face in water
That was never rained or run
I dried it with a towel
That was neither wove nor spun.

In a marble hall
As white as milk
Lined with a skin
As soft as silk
Within a fountain
Crystal clear
A golden apple doth appear
No doors there are to this
stronghold
Yet thieves break in to steal
the gold.

PHILIP BLYTHE '92

LOT NO
29

❦

Two legs on the ground
And three legs overhead
And the head of the living
In the mouth of the dead.

Neither fish nor flesh
Nor feathers nor bone
But still has fingers
And thumbs of its own.

PHILIP BLYTHE '92

As I went through yon guttery gap
I met a wee man in gay red cap
A stick in his stern and a stone
in his belly
Riddle me that and I'll give
you a penny.

Hink! Hank! On the bank
Ten drawing four.

PHILIP BLYTHE '92

17·52
2·00
18·30
12·00
7·51
23·59
V VI VII VIII

A hard-working father
And an easygoing mother
Twelve little children
As black as one another.

As round as an apple
As deep as a pail
She'll never bawl out
Till she's caught by the tail.

LINEN
IRISH LINEN

CILL CHOMHGHAILL
KILCOOLE 7
NEWCASTLE 5
RATHNEW
CILL MANNTÁIN
WICKLOW 3
GREYSTONES
BRAY 15

Hicky Picky locked the gate
Hicky Picky locked it weel
Hicky Picky locked the gate
Without iron or steel!

Four steady standards
Four diddle diddle danders
Two lookers, two hookers
And a wig-wag.

N
W
E
S
Breezy !
Stormy
Very
Stay Indoors
Lift off
co West & Sons
est 1962

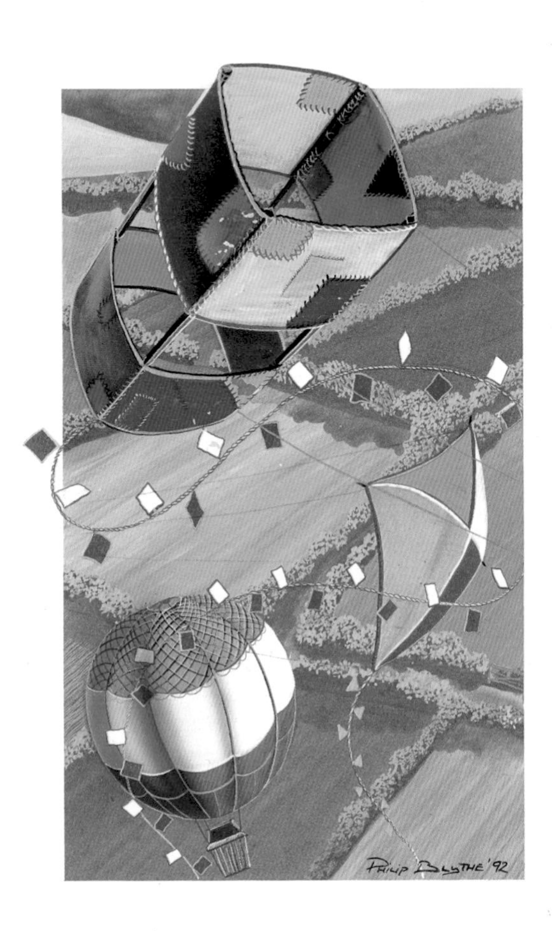
PHILIP BLYTHE '92

Patch upon patch
Without any stitches
Riddle me that
And I'll buy you some britches.

Answers

p. 4	A needle and a finger with a thimble
p. 7	The sun
p. 8	A blackberry
p. 11	A rainbow
p. 12	A pot
p. 15	A sod of turf
p. 16	A pair of boots
p. 19	A potato
p. 20	A broken egg
p. 23	A moth
p. 24	Oneself
p. 27	Wash in the dew
	Dry in the sun
p. 28	An egg
p. 31	A man with his head in a pot
p. 32	A glove
p. 35	A haw
p. 36	A man milking a cow
p. 39	A clock face
p. 40	A bell
p. 43	Frost
p. 44	A cow
p. 47	A cabbage